Collaborating for

EDITED BY PEGGY HOLMAN AND TOM DEVANE

The Whole Systems Approach

CINDY ADAMS
AND W. A. (BILL) ADAMS

BERRETT
BK COMMUNICATIONS
KOEHLER

Copyright © 1999 by Cindy Adams and W. A. (Bill) Adams

All rights reserved. No part of this publication may be reproduced, distributed, or transmitted in any form or by any means, including photocopying, recording, or other electronic or mechanical method, without the prior written permission of the publisher, except in the case of brief quotations embodied in critical reviews. For permissions requests, write to the publisher, addressed "Attention: Permissions Coordinator," at the address below:

Berrett-Koehler Communications, Inc.
450 Sansome Street, Suite 1200
San Francisco, CA 94111-3320

ORDERING INFORMATION

Please send orders to Berrett-Koehler Communications, P.O. Box 565, Williston, VT 05495. Or place your order by calling 800-929-2929, faxing 802-864-7626, or visiting www.bkconnection.com.
Special discounts are available on quantity purchases. For details, call 800-929-2929. See the back of this booklet for more information and an order form.

Printed in the United States of America
on acid-free and recycled paper.

CONTENTS

Introduction   1
    Voices That Count: Realizing the Potential of Change
    Peggy Holman and Tom Devane

The Whole Systems Approach^{SM}   7
    The Basics—What Is the Whole Systems Approach?   9
    Getting Started   16
    Roles, Responsibilities, and Relationships   19
    Impact on Power and Authority   19
    Attributes for Success   20
    Theoretical Basis   21
    Sustaining the Results   22
    Key Distinctions and Common Misconceptions   23

Notes   25

Resources   26
    Where to Go for More Information

Questions for Thinking Aloud   29

The Authors   31

INTRODUCTION

Voices That Count: Realizing the Potential of Change

. . . .
Peggy Holman and Tom Devane

As seen through the lens of history, change is inevitable. Just look at any history book. Everything from fashions to attitudes has changed dramatically through the years. Change reflects underlying shifts in values and expectations of the times. Gutenberg's invention of the movable type printing press in the fifteenth century, for example, bolstered the developing humanism of the Renaissance. The new technology complemented the emerging emphasis on individual expression that brought new developments in music, art, and literature. Economic and political shifts paralleled the changing tastes in the arts, creating a prosperous and innovative age—a stark contrast to the preceding Middle Ages.

On the surface, technology enables greater freedom and prosperity. Yet this century has overwhelmed us with new technologies: automobiles, airplanes, radios, televisions, telephones, computers, the Internet. What distinguishes change today is the turbulence created by the breathtaking pace required to assimilate its effects.

In terms of social change, one trend is clear: people are demanding a greater voice in running their own lives. Demonstrated by the American Revolution and affirmed more recently in the fall of the Berlin Wall, the riots in Tiananmen Square, the social unrest in Indonesia, and the redistribution of power in South Africa, this dramatic shift in values and expectations creates enormous potential for positive change today.

So, why does change have such a bad reputation?

One reason is that change introduces uncertainty. While change holds the possibility of good things happening, 80 percent of us see only its negative aspects.[1] And even when people acknowledge their current situation is far from perfect, given the choice between the devil they know or the devil they don't, most opt for the former. The remedy we are learning is to involve people in creating a picture of a better future. Most of us are drawn toward the excitement and possibility of change and move past our fear of the unknown.

Another reason we are wary of change is that it can create winners and losers. Clearly the British were not happy campers at the end of the American Revolution. In corporations, similar battle lines are often drawn between those with something to lose and those with something to gain. The real challenge is to view the change *systemically* and ask what's best for both parties in the post-change environment.

Finally, many people have real data that change is bad for them. These change survivors know that "flavor of the month" change initiatives generally fall disappointingly short. In our organizations and communities, many people have experienced the results of botched attempts at transformational change. Like the cat that jumps on a hot stove only once, it's simple human nature to avoid situations that cause pain. And let's face it, enough change efforts have failed to create plenty of cynicism over the past ten years. For these people, something had better "smell" completely different if they're going to allow themselves to care.

Ironically, as demands for greater involvement in our organizations increased, leaders of many well-publicized, large-scale change efforts moved the other way and totally ignored people. They chose instead to focus on more visible and seemingly easier-to-manage components such as information technology, strategic architectures, and business processes. Indeed, "Downsize" was a ubiquitous battle cry of the nineties. According to a 1996 *New York Times* poll, "Nearly three-quarters of all households have had a close encounter with layoffs since 1980. In one-third of all households, a family member has lost a job, and nearly 40 percent more know a relative, friend, or neighbor who was laid off."[2] The individual impact has been apparent in the increased stress, longer working hours, and reduced sense of job security chronicled in virtually every recent book and article on change.

To paraphrase Winston Churchill, "Never before in the field of human endeavors was so much screwed up by so few for so many." By ignoring the need to involve people in something that affects them, many of today's popular change methods have left a bad taste in the mouths of "change targets" (as one popular methodology calls those affected) for *any* type of change. They have also often left behind less effective organizations with fewer people and lower morale. Consequently, even well-intentioned, well-designed change efforts have a hard time getting off the ground.

If an organization or community's leaders *do* recognize that emerging values and rapidly shifting environmental demands call for directly engaging people in change, they often face another challenge. When the fear of uncertainty, the potential for winners and losers, and the history of failures define change, how can they systematically involve people and have some confidence that it will work? That is where this booklet comes in.

A Way Through

This booklet offers an approach that works because it acknowledges the prevailing attitudes toward change. It offers a fresh view based on the possibility of a more desirable future, experience with the whole system, and activities that signal "something different is happening this time." That difference systematically taps the potential of human beings to make themselves, their organizations, and their communities more adaptive and more effective. This approach is based on solid, proven principles for unleashing people's creativity, knowledge, and spirit toward a common purpose.

How can this be? It does so by filling two huge voids that most large-scale change efforts miss. The first improvement is *intelligently involving people* in changing their workplaces and communities. We have learned that creating a collective sense of purpose, sharing information traditionally known only to a few, valuing what people have to contribute, and inviting them to participate in meaningful ways positively affects outcomes. In other words, informed, engaged people can produce dramatic results.

The second improvement is a *systemic* approach to change. By asking "Who's affected? Who has a stake in this?" we begin to recognize that no change happens in isolation. Making the interdependencies explicit enables shifts based on a common view of the whole. We can each play our part while understanding our contribution to the system. We begin to understand that in a change effort the "one-party-wins-and-one-party-loses" perception need not necessarily be the case. When viewed from a systemic perspective, the lines between "winners" and "losers" become meaningless as everyone participates in cocreating the future for the betterment of all. The advantages are enormous: coordinated actions and closer relationships lead to simpler, more effective solutions.

The growing numbers of success stories are beginning to attract attention. Hundreds of examples around the world of dramatic and sustained increases in organization and community performance now exist.[3] With such great potential, why isn't everyone operating this way? The catch with high-involvement, systemic change is that more people have their say. Until traditional managers are ready to say yes to that, no matter how stunning the achievements of others, these approaches will remain out of reach for most and a competitive advantage for a few.

Our Purpose

This booklet describes an approach that has helped others achieve dramatic, sustainable results in their organization or communities. Our purpose is to provide basic information that you can use to decide whether this approach is right for you. We give you an overview including an illustrative story, answers to frequently asked questions and tips for getting started. We've also given you discussion questions for "thinking aloud" with others and a variety of references to learn more.

There is ample evidence that when high involvement and a system-wide approach are used, the potential for unimagined results is within reach. As Goethe so eloquently reminds us, "Whatever you can do or dream you can, begin it. Boldness has genius, power, and magic in it."

What are you waiting for?

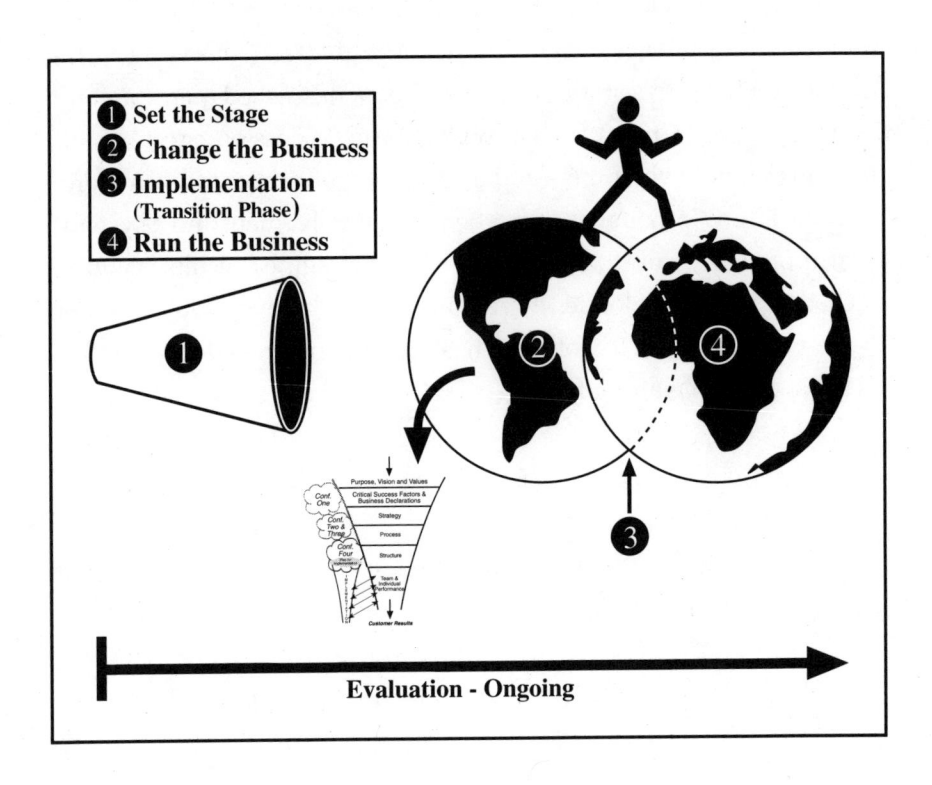

- **① Set the Stage**
- **② Change the Business**
- **③ Implementation** (Transition Phase)
- **④ Run the Business**

Evaluation - Ongoing

The Whole Systems Approach

*I don't like work—no person does—but I like what is in work—
the chance to find yourself.*
—Joseph Conrad

MichCon is a 150-year-old gas-distribution company headquartered in Detroit serving more than 500 communities throughout Michigan. In 1989, MichCon was the nation's sixth-largest local distribution company. By all measures, MichCon had been successful for years. However, Steve Ewing, CEO and president, was concerned that MichCon, historically heavily regulated, would not be able to compete when deregulation became a reality.

MichCon management was top-heavy. Activities and functions occurred in "silos"; supervisors had narrow spans of control and few people below the executive level made decisions. Employees were reluctant to assume risks, speak out, or involve themselves. Over the years, employees had become adept at following directions and doing what they were instructed to do and little more.

As Ewing observed, "We had mastered all the tools available to us and knew the next level of performance had to come through people. We wanted to increase employee satisfaction and performance while keeping the customer at the center of our universe. One conventional way to reorganize a company was to lock the vice presidents in a room and 'just do it.' We'd used that approach in the past. This time, we opted for an approach that engaged the entire organization."

In January 1990, MichCon kicked off a high-involvement process (still in place today) to continually reposition itself as the "premier" organization in its industry, based on the perception of its 1.2 million customers. MichCon committed to reinvesting in its employees, ensuring that everyone understood deregulation's impact and was aligned with a shared vision, values, and customer focus.

To help accomplish its objectives, MichCon conducted a series of large-group conferences. Over five months, approximately 300 employees, representing all levels of the organization, participated in each conference. Ten percent of the participants repeated to ensure continuity between conferences. During each conference, the rest of the organization received daily updates via MCTV (the in-house television channel) and news releases. When each conference was completed, participants carried key messages back to the organization. All employees helped create input for the next conference. In this way, the entire company actively participated, with employees adding their voices to decisions whether they were "in the room" or not.

As of 1998, MichCon continued to be one of the most profitable U.S. utilities. The company's operations and maintenance budget is significantly less than when the effort was launched—proof that employees are working more effectively than in the past. The employee population has dropped from 4,200 to 2,800, all through natural attrition, while the company has added 20,000 customers per year. The company has earned its highest-ever customer satisfaction rating—100 percent in five groups and a 92 percent average in the others. Ewing attributes all of this to the foundation that was established to transform the company ahead of its time.

MichCon's efforts would not have been successful had Ewing been an episodic, activity-driven leader. Given Ewing's admitted impatience, his demonstrated commitment to the long term and involving everyone was an anchor for others. "We'd tried a lot of changes, some of which worked, some of which didn't," Ewing confided to an audience of utility executives in February 1997: "From my perspective, the single most significant accomplishment was changing the company's course and basing its guidance system on the shift from regulation to competition."

The Basics—What Is the Whole Systems Approach?

At the highest level, the Whole Systems Approach[SM] is a model for transforming any business into a thriving organization by aligning internal systems with external forces and engaging the hearts and minds of every person. It is *sustainable* because the approach is used to run the business long after changes have been implemented. At this level, the Whole Systems Approach is a model for organizational effectiveness.

The name itself—*whole systems*—goes to the core of the approach. Every necessary system within the organization is created, modified, or redesigned and then integrated and aligned. Every stakeholder—employees, suppliers, and *customers*—is involved.

This approach is grounded in practicality. As practitioners, we have learned what works and what can work inside organizations. The Whole Systems Approach is particularly valuable when

- a need to fundamentally change exists;
- a system or process is not running effectively or optimally;
- creating a new possibility adds significant value;
- current efforts are not on track—they lack speed, results, or broad ownership.

This integrated approach accomplishes two critical tasks:

1. It brings maximum experience and wisdom to the table and in a remarkably short time turns that experience and wisdom into action. It creates new, aligned systems, goals, roles, procedures, and sustainable results.

2. It accelerates employee commitment and ownership of change by involving all stakeholders in decisions.

The Conference Process Within the Whole Systems Approach: An Overview

The Whole Systems Approach evolved over the last 15 years as we worked with organizations on large-scale change initiatives. With the methods developed, integrated, and refined, we have reduced the cycle time for large-scale efforts from 7 years to 24–30 months. Improvements to this approach have been primarily achieved using innovation, full-participation strategies, and technologies such as large-group conferencing.

The process begins by clarifying the business imperative and reasons for change. Once the decision to proceed is made, the entire organization participates in a series of conferences involving 60 to 600 or more people, as well as interconference activities (see Table 1).

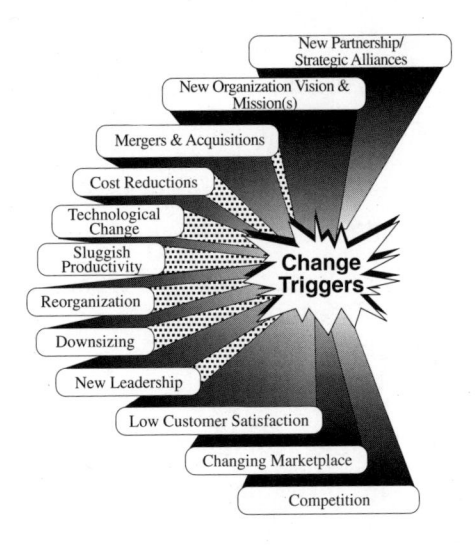

Figure 1. Many Situations Trigger the Need for Major Change

The whole system is involved, connecting to the people and information developed during conferences, confirming the findings, creating the products for the next steps, and ratifying the decisions reached.

This approach leverages the time and resource investment to build a cohesive whole. By being persistent (following through) and consistent, an organization can transform itself and acquire the competency to be "change-able." The business now runs using the same approach it used to change. This resulting capability for rapid change with a responsible and aligned workforce is a significant competitive advantage.

Flow	*Time Frame and Activities*
Conference 1	The first two- or three-day conference focuses on the *company's future:* purpose, vision, and values; business imperative; and customers. Following the conference, people begin redefining the systems of organizational effectiveness (leadership, communications, measurement, delivery, accountability, and human performance).
Conference 2	The second conference is three days. It focuses on the *strategy,* core busiess processes, and customer requirements. The measurement system begins to take shape following the second conference.
Conference 3	During the one or two days of the third conference, participants work to understand and integrate *processes.* The between-conference work includes developing structure possibilities.
Conference 4	During the fourth conference, which is usually three days, the structure is set and a comprehensive implementation plan is developed.
Implementation	Implementation follows, involving many one-day miniconferences for developing process, unit, and team details. Periodic integration summits keep people informed about progress and connected to the overall picture.

Table 1. The Conference Process

Business Imperative/Reason for Change
(Stakeholder Input, Feedback, etc.)

- Conference One
  - Purpose, Vision, and Values
  - Critical Success Factors and Business Declarations
- Conferences Two and Three
  - Strategy
  - Process
- Conference Four / Plan for Implementation
  - Structure
  - Team and Individual Performance

IMPLEMENTATION

Stakeholder Results

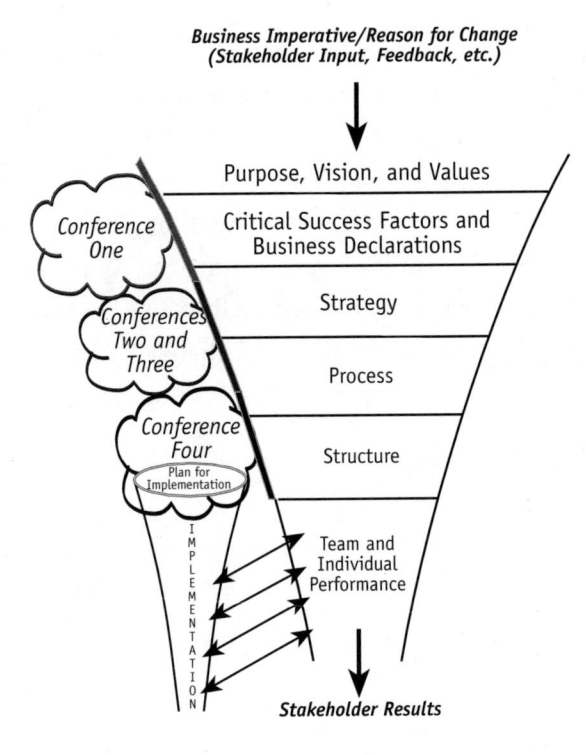

Figure 2. Whole Systems Approach Conference Flow

Probable Outcomes

The Whole Systems Approach can

- achieve successful, fundamental change and "corporate reinvention";
- create a resilient, flexible organization while accelerating the speed of traditional organizational change by a multiple of four;
- produce outstanding results that could not have been accomplished using traditional approaches;
- build organizational self-reliance and foster an environment conducive to sustaining a thriving organization and a successful future;

- develop stakeholders who are involved, aligned, and committed to the success of the organization.

Whole Systems Approach Framework

The conference flow described earlier occurs within a larger context. It is based on four different views of the organization:

Component	Focus	Orientation	Purpose	Indicators
Seven Conditions of Thriving Organizations	Condition	Living, organic	To understand the overall health of the system	Vital signs
Alignment Model	Alignment	Vertical	To understand the linkages in the system, from the general to the specific	Line-of-sight associations
Six Systems of Organizational Effectiveness	Systems	Horizontal	To understand the cross-functional connections in the system	Interconnections
Whole System Phases of Transformation	Process	Progressive	To understand the sequential flow of events through the transformation of the system	Time

Table 2. Four Views of the Organizations

The Seven Conditions acknowledge the unseen, internal health of the organization. The Alignment Model establishes an organization's essential nature. The Six Systems define its operations. And the Phases of Transformation tell the story of the organization's journey through the process.

Seven Conditions of Thriving Organizations

Through study, research, and practical experience, we have identified seven conditions consistently present in thriving organizations. The major role of senior leaders is to create and foster these conditions:

- *Information:* the lifeblood flowing through and nourishing the entire organization,
- *Participation:* the key factor in the organization's potential for limitless possibilities,
- *Relationships:* the context for results within the organization,
- *Adaptability:* the organization's ability to respond to changing conditions,
- *Creativity:* the organization's renewal capacity for infusing new energy and results,
- *Interconnectedness:* the threads that make up the fabric of interdependence throughout the organization,
- *Identity:* the DNA that connects the organization's past and future in the present.

When these conditions are weak or absent, the organization can become diseased and sluggish. When physicians perform a physical, they focus on the vital signs. The Seven Conditions are the vital signs of a living organization.

Alignment Model: Creating and Ensuring "Line of Sight" to the Customer

When individuals and the organization are aligned, there is more trust. Crucial to this premise is a legitimate voice for every employee in every critical area, such as how work is accomplished and decisions are made.

The Alignment Model provides a path to achieving customer results. The top of the funnel is wide to allow maximum input and a scan of all information. Working down the funnel, alignment becomes more focused, moving from the global to the specific and from the organization to the individual. At the funnel's bottom, participation is clearly visible in individual contribution, the results achieved, and direct line of sight to the customer.

THE WHOLE SYSTEMS APPROACH 15

Business Imperative/Reason for Change
(Stakeholder Input, Feedback, etc.)

↓

Purpose, Vision, and Values

Critical Success Factors and Business Declarations

Strategy

Process

Structure

Team and Individual Performance

↓

Stakeholder Results

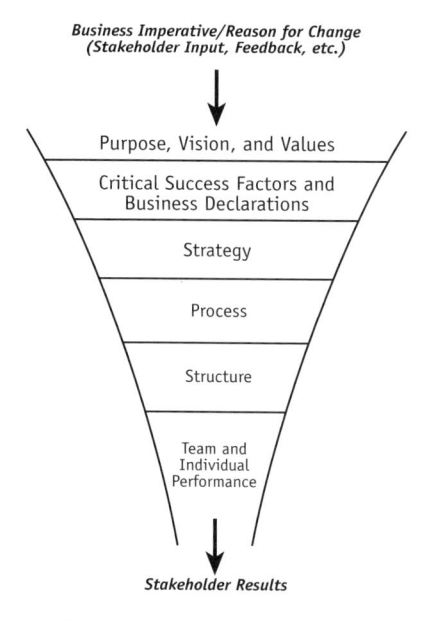

Figure 3. The Alignment Model

Six Systems of Organizational Effectiveness

Inherent potential—a latent and unique capacity for greatness—exists within every organization. Far from automatic, this potential must be coaxed to the surface before it can emerge and nurtured before it can thrive. Each system is vital for organization effectiveness and self-reliance. This simple operating frame helps organization members understand how everything is integrated and what is important for success. As with the Alignment Model, the Six Systems operate at the macro level (organization-wide) and the micro level (project, departmental, or individual).

Whole System Phases of Transformation

The fourth component describes actions in sequential, time-bound phases. The phases apply regardless of where the organization is in the process. Sometimes the phases are a road map to unite a transformation

The Six Systems Diagram

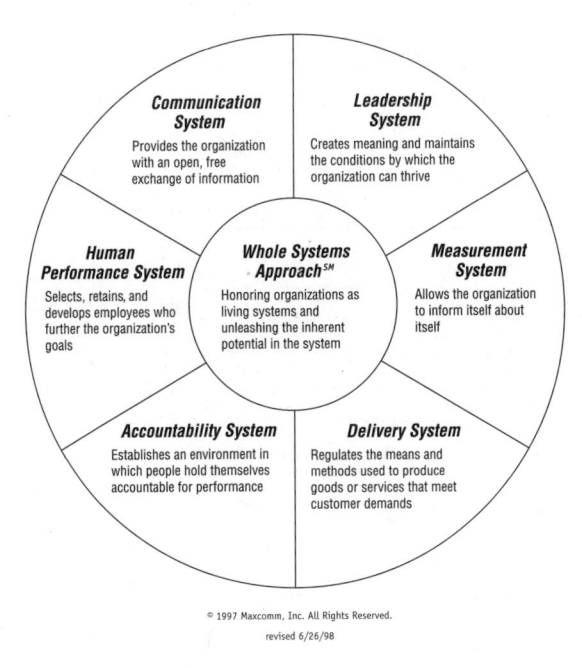

- **Communication System**: Provides the organization with an open, free exchange of information
- **Leadership System**: Creates meaning and maintains the conditions by which the organization can thrive
- **Measurement System**: Allows the organization to inform itself about itself
- **Delivery System**: Regulates the means and methods used to produce goods or services that meet customer demands
- **Accountability System**: Establishes an environment in which people hold themselves accountable for performance
- **Human Performance System**: Selects, retains, and develops employees who further the organization's goals
- **Whole Systems Approach℠** (center): Honoring organizations as living systems and unleashing the inherent potential in the system

© 1997 Maxcomm, Inc. All Rights Reserved.
revised 6/26/98

Figure 4. The Six Systems

effort already in progress. In other instances, the phases launch a new initiative. Regardless of the effort's status, honoring and capitalizing on existing good work establishes respect and avoids duplication.

Table 3 shows the general actions that occur within each phase.

Getting Started

Before beginning, ensure that

1. the senior leader is committed to the work and has a trusted, skilled change partner (internal or external),
2. the expertise to safely navigate through the required changes is available,
3. the change approach is aligned and consistent with running the business long term,
4. necessary change agents and leaders are committed to the approach prior to kickoff.

Phase	Primary Actions
Set the Stage	• Develop senior leadership commitment and ownership • Prepare the organization for change
Change the Business	• Move the organization through the Alignment Model using the conferencing process • Develop the Seven Conditions and Six Systems • Engage in personal and team development designed to unfreeze old behaviors
Transition the Business (Implementation)	• Prepare the organization to live in two worlds at once • Prepare leadership for the enormous focus, resiliency, and persistence required • Ensure the Six Systems are fully functional
Run the Business	• Nourish the Seven Conditions; ensure the organization is thriving • Ensure dedicated resources to sustain system effectiveness • Continue using the Alignment Model and Six Systems at the micro level to develop effective teams

Table 3. Phases of Transformation

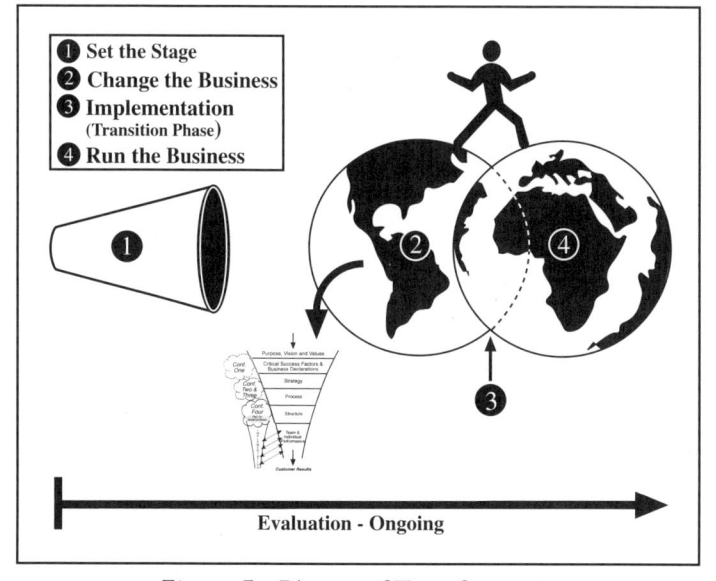

Figure 5. Phases of Transformation

	Before	During	After
Leader	• Commits to change • Makes all strategic and many tactical decisions • Directs employees; plans work; controls work and workers • Evaluates productivity	• Demonstrates commitment • Lets go of control • Builds broad base of leadership • Sponsors teams; delegates sponsorship to others • Models and reinforces; is highly visible • Provides "big picture" context and ensures "meaning for change" • Makes decisions with the organization	• Continues to demonstrate commitment • Sponsors teams with other members • Makes decisions with organization • Assumes accountability for enterprise results versus micromanaging tactical units • Ensures Seven Conditions for health • Continues to provide "big picture" context and direction
Consultant/ Designer/ Facilitator	• Secures leader commitment • Assesses current situation • Oversees design and transformation planning • Educates leaders and others involved	• Partners with organization to achieve results • Oversees design of conferencing process • Trains internal facilitators if more are needed	• Transfers skills, when possible, to others • Helps assess results and identify next steps • Continues to act as a guide
Employee/ Participant	• Works only in immediate area • Follows orders from leaders • Feels "less than" accountable, responsible, or fully utilized	• Participates fully • Voices ideas • Lets "old baggage" go • Makes decisions with leadership about how the company will operate	• Operates from a process-oriented, team-based view • Plans and controls work • Evaluates productivity • Acts as decision maker in all areas affecting work • Adopts new behaviors/competencies • Accepts personal responsibility and accountability

Table 4. Roles, Responsibilities, and Relationships

Roles, Responsibilities, and Relationships

Initially, leadership commitment ensures organizational resources and guidance for the transformation. Over time, organization-wide commitment is required. For a broad-based organizational effort, top management must be actively involved, modeling desired behavior.

Internal and external facilitators contribute to the process. External resources often provide objective perspectives and experience. At a minimum, external facilitators can help ground and align leadership. The ratio of external to internal facilitators depends on the capacity, competencies, and credibility of internal resources. Whenever possible, use internal resources.

Impact on Power and Authority

Because the Whole Systems Approach is a total involvement strategy of planned, not episodic, change, all organization members are participants. Significant shifts in roles and structure occur using this approach. Most notably, after the first conference, employees realize they have a legitimate voice in making decisions and are much more willing to take responsibility and accountability. Shifts continue throughout the change and transition phases. This approach is not about "someone doing something to us"; rather, "we are doing it to ourselves." Roles become more team-based, process-oriented, and results-driven. Leadership shifts include the following:

From	To
Disconnected from the whole	Strategic direction mobilizers, meaning creators, integrators
Managers	Coaches, facilitators
Day-to-day project leaders	High-level leaders

Table 5. Leadership Shifts

Attributes for Success

Initially, the Whole Systems Approach requires one involved, persistent leader. Over time, it requires commitment to stay with the effort. Without this base, this approach will fail to produce the desired outcomes.

This approach changes the way we think about and do our work. Attributes for success include

- personal, courageous leadership and focused energy from the top;
- engaged, talented people—hearts and minds;
- whole systems perspective and action;
- comprehensive implementation plan including dedicated resources—time, people, and money;
- business imperative for change—creating a sense of urgency to change;
- obsession to meet or exceed customer/stakeholder expectations;
- understanding of the market and competition;
- measures that drive performance.

Following are some important points to remember when using this approach:

Do . . .	Don't . . .
Make the commitment and do the work	Believe this approach is a panacea
Plan and deploy well	Neglect planning; this leads to ineffective deployment
Ensure the time and resources are available for people to develop the skills they need	Forget to plan for organizational capacity issues and resource constraints
Expect accountability everywhere	Delegate accountability away from senior leadership
Pay attention to specifics	Forget that "the devil is in the details"

Table 6. Do's and Don'ts

Theoretical Basis

This approach evolved over the last 15 years because we believe in the inherent potential of living systems. People typically report that less than 30 percent of their capability is used at work. That means 70 percent of the organization's latent human capacity is dormant and untapped. To access this potential, we began experimenting with creating common values and systems through broad-based participation.

In 1991 we were several years into two major change efforts. Based on client results and feedback, both efforts were going well. Our models had been refined and proven in the field over the previous seven years. Yet we knew that 70 percent of people's potential remained untapped. We decided to conduct further research, apply new ideas, and redesign accordingly. Shortly thereafter, we began working with Meg Wheatley and joint-ventured the first two Self-Organizing Systems Conferences.

Our research included exploring

- applications of chaos and complexity theories;
- measurement systems, especially balanced scorecard applications;
- application of quality technologies;
- process-improvement applications (Geary Rummler and Alan Brache);
- Sociotechnical Systems (William Pasmore and others);
- Fred Emery and Eric Trist's Search applications;
- Marvin Weisbord's *Discovering Common Ground;*
- Margaret Wheatley's work in self-organizing systems;
- Michael Hammer and James Champy's work in reengineering.

We searched for "what works." The search led us into an in-depth study of living systems, chaos theory, self-organizing systems, and complexity and process-redesign theories, with an emphasis on creating practical, outcome-based measures. We commissioned an independent research firm to review current literature and assess the strengths and weaknesses of various organizational change approaches.

Our approach is deeply rooted in and a blend of what we studied. It has one fundamental difference that is based on our experience: organizations are living systems with mechanical parts that must be aligned and honored for the enterprise to thrive. This approach is not exclusive but rather inclusive. It capitalizes on the synergy birthed through integration. It recognizes what works in the organization's operating system. We have learned that integration is a key requirement for shifting from inherent potential to manifesting organizational potential. It is integration that unlocks the potential for people to thrive at work and create incredible organizational results.

We believe that substantial, permanent leaps in bottom-line productivity will not come from new technology or products. Competition replicates these sooner or later. Breakthrough productivity comes through winning the hearts and minds of the people. Relationships are an appreciating asset and the new paradigm for realizing results.

Sustaining the Results

The Whole Systems Approach runs the business long after the changes are in place, creating sustainable results and organizational self-reliance. This is a significant distinction because once a change effort runs its course, it is often cast aside as an aberration. The company goes "back to normal." In contrast, this approach becomes part of the organization's DNA. It balances outstanding business results with valuing people and replicating processes.

For enduring results from the "Run the Business" phase, focus on

- *ensuring that "running" the business is consistent with "changing" the business.* If large-group participation is used to change the business, then use participation to run the business.

- *building organizational self-reliance.* Once implementation is complete, the focus shifts to reinforcing and sustaining the new behaviors and systems, building the core competence of self-reliance. For instance, if common tools, templates, and practices are consistently used, people learn to apply them in a variety of situations.
- *sustaining resource capacity.* The same focus on resources used to change the business must be maintained to run the business. Once a system is running, many people think it can run on its own. This is rarely the case.

Key Distinctions and Common Misconceptions

The key distinctions of the Whole Systems Approach are twofold:

- focusing on running the business once the changes have been accomplished,
- treating organizations as living systems with mechanical parts, not one or the other.

Other distinctions include the following:

- not episodic or event driven but rather outcome driven with a focus on the long term and organizational integration,
- not a conferencing method but rather an integrated approach using a variety of methods and strategies to ensure full participation and commitment,
- an overall framework for integration and results that can be stand-alone or coupled with other efforts and initiatives.

Common misconceptions about this approach include the following:

- *This is a one-time event.* Often the belief persists that if we can just get through this situation, business will go "back to normal" or "we can get back to work." This approach fundamentally changes the running of the business.

- *Participation ensures results.* Participation, and particularly large-group conferencing, does not guarantee that results will follow.
- *The need for management and leadership is eliminated.* To the contrary, the paradox is that as organizational members assume more accountability and responsibility, stronger leadership is required to ensure success.
- *Involving customers is not necessary.* Customers are essential to this process. Many times, companies fear involving stakeholders; however, every time stakeholders are included, an authentic "win-win" situation results.
- *It is not leader dependent.* As much as we would like to believe that broad organizational change occurs without the CEO's or senior leader's involvement and commitment, it does not.
- *Increased energy is not required.* Changing an organization consumes tremendous energy and demands persistence. The personal fortitude and commitment to see an effort through is both taxing and exhilarating!

Notes

[1] Oakley, Ed, and Doug Krug. *Enlightened Leadership.* Denver, Colo.: Stone Tree Publishing, 1991, p. 38.

[2] The *New York Times, The Downsizing of America.* New York: Times Books, 1996.

[3] Holman, Peggy, and Tom Devane, eds. *The Change Handbook: Group Methods for Shaping the Future.* San Francisco: Berrett-Koehler Publishers, 1999. This book contains over twenty such stories of stellar results from high-involvement, systemic change.

RESOURCES

Where to Go for More Information

. . . .

Since our focus has been to give you an *introduction* to the Whole Systems Approach, we want you to know where to go for more information. Here are books, articles, Web sites, and other sources that can help you develop a more in-depth understanding. In addition, we have provided recommendations of works that have influenced us.

Organization

Maxcomm, Inc.
Cindy Adams or Bill Adams
4766 South Holladay Blvd. #200
Salt Lake City, UT 84117
(800) 767-5212 or (801) 273-1776
(801) 273-1845 (fax)
Maxcommail@aol.com (e-mail)
www.maxcomminc.com (Web site)

- Public workshops and customized seminars
- Maxcomm videos of large-group conferences and the Voice of the Customer
- *Connections,* a quarterly newsletter published by Maxcomm, Inc.

The Whole Systems Approach References

For an extended reading list, call Maxcomm, Inc., or visit our Web site.

Cindy Adams, W. A. (Bill) Adams, with Michael Bowker. *The Whole Systems Approach Involving Everyone in the Company to Transform and Run Your Business.* Provo, Utah: Executive Excellence Publishing, 1999.

Maxcomm's Whole Systems Approach[SM] *to Changing and Running Your Business Guide.* Salt Lake City, Utah: Maxcomm, Inc., 1999.

A comprehensive "how-to" manual documenting the entire changing and running-the-business process from a Whole Systems Approach perspective. The purpose of the guide is to create "a world of work where people thrive."

Influential Sources

Block, Peter. *Stewardship: Choosing Service over Self-Interest.* San Francisco: Berrett-Koehler, 1993.

Bunker, B., and B. Alban. *Large Group Interventions: Engaging the Whole System for Rapid Change.* San Francisco: Jossey-Bass, 1997.

Collins, James C., and Jerry I. Porras. *Built to Last: Successful Habits of Visionary Companies.* New York: HarperCollins, 1997.

Jacobs, Robert W. *Real Time Strategic Change: How to Involve an Entire Organization in Fast and Far-Reaching Change.* San Francisco: Berrett-Koehler, 1994.

Hamel, Gary, and C. K. Prahalad. *Competing for the Future: Breakthrough Strategies for Seizing Control of Your Industry and Creating the Markets of Tomorrow.* Boston: Harvard Business School Press, 1994.

Hammer, Michael, and James Champy. *Reengineering the Corporation: A Manifesto for Business Revolution.* New York: HarperCollins, 1994.

Kaplan, Robert S., and David P. Norton. *The Balanced Scorecard: Translating Strategy into Action.* Boston: Harvard Business School Press, 1996.

Pasmore, William A. *Creating Strategic Change: Designing the Flexible, High-Performing Organization.* Somerset, N.J.: John Wiley & Sons, 1994.

Peck, M. Scott. *The Different Drum: Community Making and Peace; A Spiritual Journey Toward Self-Acceptance, True Belonging, and New Hope for the World.* New York: Touchstone, 1987.

Rummler, Geary A., and Alan P. Brache. *Improving Performance: How to Manage the White Space in the Organizational Chart.* San Francisco: Jossey-Bass Management Series, 1995.

Senge, Peter M. *The Fifth Discipline: The Art & Practice of the Learning Organization,* New York: Currency Doubleday, 1990.

Weisbord, Marvin R. *Discovering Common Ground: How Future Search Conferences Bring People Together to Achieve Breakthrough Innovation, Empowerment, Shared Vision and Collaborative Action.* San Francisco: Berrett-Koehler, 1992.

———. *Productive Workplaces: Organizing and Managing for Dignity, Meaning, and Community.* San Francisco: Jossey-Bass, 1987. Presents a conceptual and historical framework for organizational change and work design.

Wheatley, Margaret J. *Leadership and the New Science: Learning About Organization from an Orderly Universe.* San Francisco: Berrett-Koehler, 1992.

Questions for Thinking Aloud

The following questions are designed to facilitate discussion and assist in determining if the Whole Systems Approach is a methodology that could work for your organization.

1. What aspects of the Whole Systems Approach appear to be similar to other approaches your organization has used in the past? How is this approach different? What aspects of past efforts worked for you? Which ones did not? Why?

2. What benefits do you anticipate your organization could realize by using an approach that involves everyone in changing and running your business?

3. What is needed for the Whole Systems Approach to be successful in your organization? Who should sponsor the effort? How would you present the idea to that person? Who should be in on the "should we or shouldn't we" conversation?

4. How do you see the Whole Systems Approach aligning with the way your organization currently operates? Who is likely to support such an effort? Who is likely to resist? What is each person's stake? Why?

The Whole Systems Approach provides a highly integrated framework for changing and running a business. Assessing organizational readiness is something that is not easy to quantify. However, conducting a preliminary needs assessment can be an effective way of building commitment for change. To access a needs assessment guide, check out our Web site at www.maxcomminc.com.

The Authors

Cindy Adams is a principal of Maxcomm, Inc., an international organizational-transformation firm. Cindy specializes in organizational transformation, cultural change, work redesign, large-group conferencing, leadership coaching, team building, and customer service enhancement. She holds a master's degree in organizational management.

W. A. (Bill) Adams is a cofounder of Maxcomm, specializing in the Whole Systems Approach, organizational transformation, and cultural change. He partners with leaders to align companies to a common purpose through a total-participation strategy. He holds a master's degree in organizational communication. He coauthored the book *The Quest for Quality: Prescriptions for Achieving Service Excellence* (St. Martin's Press, 1996).

Some of Bill and Cindy's clients include Ameritech IS, Oakwood Healthcare, Kemper Insurance, Intermedia Communications, American Express, Blue Cross/Blue Shield of Florida, GOJO Industries, Mich-Con, Tupperware, 3M Health Information Services, and First Security Information Technology, Inc.

The Whole Systems Approach provides a viable alternative and tremendously exciting opportunity for any organization to become part of a legacy. It embodies the beliefs and dreams nurtured by the authors for the past 25 years. The authors hope this approach engages people in shaping a legacy so that the next generation views work as a place of joy, fulfillment, and purpose—a world of work where people thrive. They want to help guide individuals and organizations, present and future, toward realizing this deeply personal vision.

The authors want to thank Marjean Daniels for her valuable input, editing, project management, and support. This booklet would not have been complete without her.

Series Editors
Peggy Holman is a writer and consultant who helps organizations achieve cultural transformation. High involvement and a whole-systems perspective characterize her work. Her clients include AT&T Wireless Services, Weyerhaeuser Company, St. Joseph's Medical Center, and the U.S. Department of Labor. Peggy can be reached at (425) 746-6274 or pholman@msn.com.

Tom Devane is an internationally known consultant and speaker specializing in transformation. He helps companies plan and implement transformations that utilize highly participative methods to achieve sustainable change. His clients include Microsoft, Hewlett-Packard, AT&T, Johnson & Johnson, and the Republic of South Africa. Tom can be reached at (303) 898-6172 or tdevane@iex.net.

The Change Handbook

Group Methods for Shaping the Future

Edited by Peggy Holman and Tom Devane

The Change Handbook presents eighteen proven, highly successful change methods that enable organizations and communities of all shapes and sizes to engage and focus the energy and commitment of all their members These diverse participative change approaches, described in detail by their creators and expert practitioners, illustrate how organizations and communities today can achieve and sustain extraordinary results and foster a capacity to handle the inevitable turbulence along the way. By first systematically involving all organizational stakeholders in the change process, and then planning and implementing change simultaneously—in real time—these methods uniquely enable all members to become change agents, active participants in determining their organization's direction and future.

Marvin Weisbord, Merrelyn Emery, Masaaki Imai, Kathie Dannemiller, Harrison Owen, and many other leading thinkers and practitioners of organizational change show how to harness the vision, energy, and enthusiasm of the entire organization—from employees at all levels to key stakeholders to entire communities. In *The Change Handbook* they provide practical answers to frequently asked questions to that you can choose the methods that will work best in your participative change efforts.

> "In a world where change is the norm, where the effectiveness of organizations is a competitive advantage, and where we have more change methodologies available than most people could absorb in a lifetime, this book has identified how to match the best approach to the situation. While providing structured guidelines for organizational improvement, the authors acknowledge and celebrate the power of creativity and engaged people to provide the energy needed for successful change."
>
> —SUSAN MERSEREAU, *Vice President,*
> *Organizational Effectiveness, Weyerhaeuser Company*

Paperback original, approx. 450 pages, ISBN 1-57675-058-2
Item no. 50582-605   U.S. $49.95
To order call 800-929-2929 or visit www.bkconnection.com

Collaborating for Change
Peggy Holman and Tom Devane, Editors

The Collaborating for Change booklet series offers concise, comprehensive overviews of 14 leading change strategies in a convenient, inexpensive format. Adapted from chapters in *The Change Handbook*, each booklet is written by the originator of the change strategy or an expert practitioner, and includes

- An example of the strategy in action
- Tips for getting started
- An outline of roles, responsibilities, and relationships
- Conditions for success
- Keys to sustaining results
- Thought-provoking questions for discussion

If you're deciding on a change strategy for your organization and you need a short, focused treatment of several alternatives to distribute to your colleagues, or you've decided on a change strategy and want to disseminate information about it to get everyone on board, the Collaborating for Change booklets are the ideal choice.

◆ SEARCH CONFERENCE
Merrelyn Emery and Tom Devane
Uses open systems principles in strategic planning, thereby creating a well-articulated, achievable future with identifiable goals, a timetable, and action plans for realizing that future.

◆ FUTURE SEARCH
Marvin R. Weisbord and Sandra Janoff
Helps members of an organization or community discover common ground and create self-managed plans to move toward their desired future.

◆ THE CONFERENCE MODEL
Emily M. Axelrod and Richard H. Axelrod
Engages the critical mass needed for success in redesigning organizations and processes, co-creating a vision of the future, improving customer and supplier relationships, or achieving strategic alignment.

◆ THE WHOLE SYSTEMS APPROACH
Cindy Adams and W. A. (Bill) Adams
Creates a world of work where people and organizations thrive and produce outrageous individual and organizational results.

◆ PREFERRED FUTURING
Lawrence L. Lippitt
Mobilizes everyone involved in a human system to envision the future they want and then develop strategies to get there.

- **THE STRATEGIC FORUM**
Chris Soderquist
Answers "Can our strategy achieve our objectives?" by building shared understanding (a mental map) of how the organization or community really works.

- **PARTICIPATIVE DESIGN WORKSHOP**
Merrelyn Emery and Tom Devane
Enables an organization to function in an interrelated structure of self-managing work groups.

- **GEMBA KAIZEN**
Masaaki Imai and Brian Heymans
Builds a culture able to initiate and sustain change by providing skills to improve process, enabling employees to make daily improvements, installing JIT systems and lean process methods in administrative systems, and improving equipment reliability and product quality.

- **THE ORGANIZATION WORKSHOP**
Barry Oshry and Tom Devane
Develops the knowledge and skills of "system sight" that enable us to create partnerships up, down, and across organizational lines.

- **WHOLE-SCALE CHANGE**
Kathleen D. Dannemiller, Sylvia L. James, and Paul D. Tolchinsky
Helps organizations remain successful through fast, deep, and sustainable total system change by bringing members together as one-brain (all seeing the same things) and one-heart (all committed to achieving the same preferred future).

- **OPEN SPACE TECHNOLOGY**
Harrison Owen (with Anne Stadler)
Enables high levels of group interaction and productivity to provide a basis for enhanced organizational function over time.

- **APPRECIATIVE INQUIRY**
David L. Cooperrider and Diana Whitney
Supports full-voiced appreciative participation in order to tap an organization's positive change core and inspire collaborative action that serves the whole system.

- **THINK LIKE A GENIUS PROCESS**
Todd Siler
Helps individuals and organizations go beyond narrow, compartmentalized thinking; improve communication, teamwork, and collaboration; and achieve breakthrough thinking.

- **REAL TIME STRATEGIC CHANGE**
Robert W. Jacobs and Frank McKeown
Uses large, interactive group meetings to rapidly create an organization's preferred future and then sustain it over time.

Collaborating for Change Order Form
Each booklet comes shrinkwrapped in packets of 6

Order in Quantity and Save!
1–4 packets: $45 per packet • 5–9 packets: $40.50 per packet
10–49 packets: $38.25 per packet • 50–99 packets: $36 per packet

# of Packets		Item #	Price
_____	Search Conference	6058X-605	_____
_____	Future Search	60598-605	_____
_____	The Strategic Forum	60601-605	_____
_____	Participative Design Workshop	6061X-605	_____
_____	Gemba Kaizen	60628-605	_____
_____	The Whole Systems Approach	60636-605	_____
_____	Preferred Futuring	60644-605	_____
_____	The Organization Workshop	60652-605	_____
_____	Whole-Scale Change	60660-605	_____
_____	Open Space Technology	60679-605	_____
_____	Appreciative Inquiry	60687-605	_____
_____	The Conference Model	60695-605	_____
_____	Think Like a Genius Process	60709-605	_____
_____	Real Time Strategic Change	60717-605	_____

Shipping and Handling _____
($4.50 for the first packet; $1.50 for each additional packet.)

TOTAL (CA residents add sales tax) $_____

Method of Payment
Orders payable in U.S. dollars. Orders outside U.S. and Canada must be prepaid.

❏ Payment enclosed ❏ Visa ❏ MasterCard ❏ American Express

Card no. _____ Expiration date _____

Signature _____

Name _____ Title _____

Organization _____

Address _____

City/State/Zip _____

Phone (in case we have questions about your order) _____

May we notify you about new Berrett-Koehler products and special offers via e-mail?

E-mail _____

Send Orders to Berrett-Koehler Communications, Inc., P.O. Box 565, Williston, VT 05495 • **Fax** (802) 864-7626 • **Phone** (800) 929-2929 • **Web** www.bkconnection.com